TAGAKI ⑳

多書き

JN207040

TAGAKI（多書き）とは、一言で言えば、「英語で自分を表現することを学ぶための、ボルダリング競技みたいなもの」です。その足場はメンタル面と英語面の2種類で、この足場を使って登って行き頂上を目指しましょう。この TAGAKI では、考える→書く→伝えるを30トピックくり返すことで、自分の意見を持ち、英語を書けるようになります。そうすると世界に飛び出して行けそうな自分を感じることができるでしょう。

TAGAKI 20 Contents <ruby>もくじ</ruby>

進度表 終わったトピックの番号に印をつけていきましょう!

TAGAKI 20 をはじめよう

TAGAKI 20では少し文章は長くなりますが、自分1人の力でトピックの内容(ないよう)について考え、自分はどちらのタイプの人かをぱっと決めて、すらすらと書けるように練習しましょう。また、発表する機会(きかい)があれば「文字から音声へ」の理想を達成(たっせい)することができます。

進め方

Step 1 Thinking / Reading

トピックについて考えましょう。
Sample Sentences 1 2 を見て、自分は 1 2 のどちらのタイプかを決め、次に Words and Phrases A B を見ます。

Step 2 Listening

Sample Sentences と Words and Phrases の音声をQRコードできくことができます。音声をチェックしましょう。

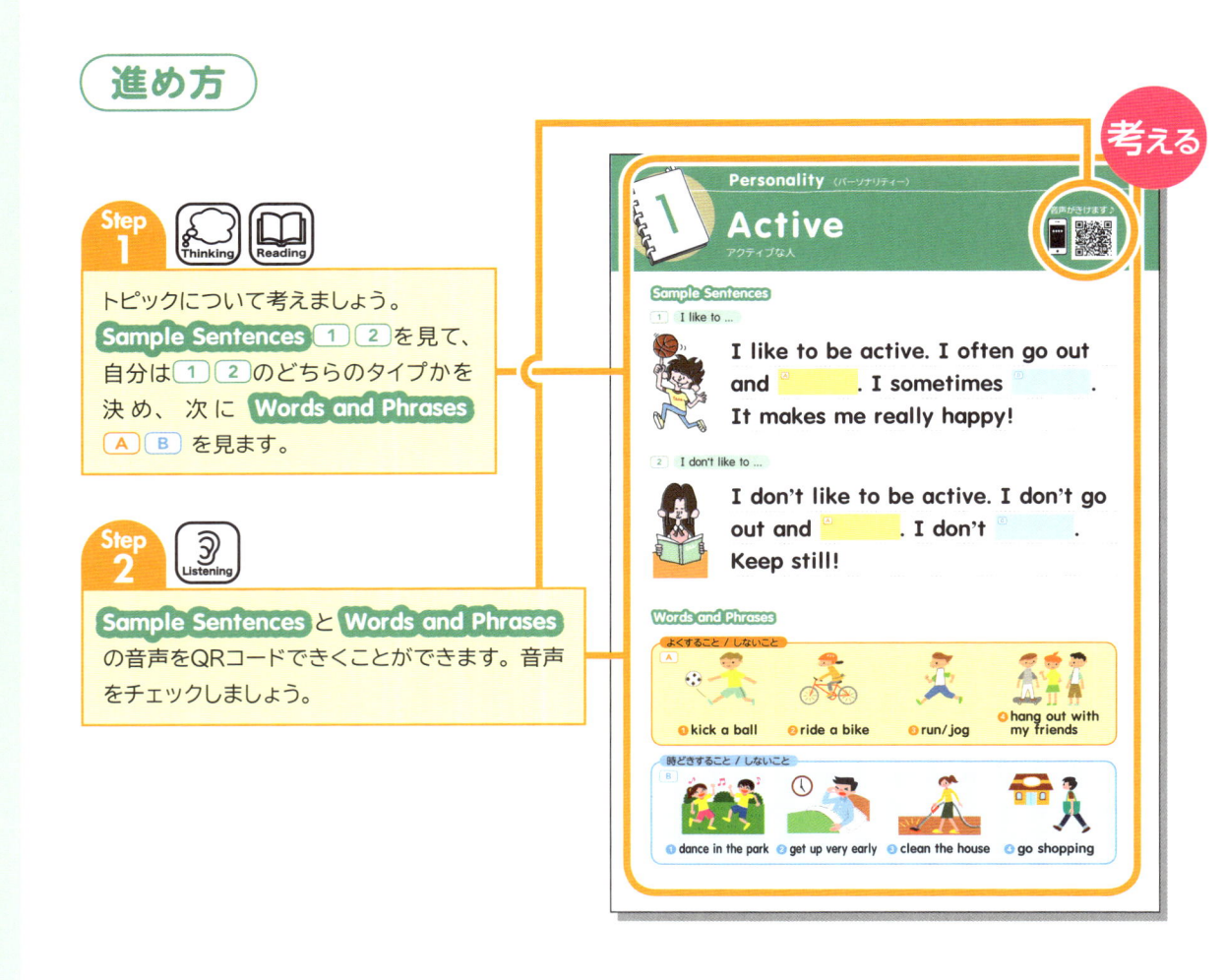

考える

Personality 〈パーソナリティー〉

1 Active
アクティブな人

音声がきけます♪

Sample Sentences

1 I like to ...

I like to be active. I often go out and _____. I sometimes _____. It makes me really happy!

2 I don't like to ...

I don't like to be active. I don't go out and _____. I don't _____. Keep still!

Words and Phrases

A よくすること / しないこと

1 kick a ball　2 ride a bike　3 run/jog　4 hang out with my friends

B 時どきすること / しないこと

1 dance in the park　2 get up very early　3 clean the house　4 go shopping

---

1人で TAGAKIを学ぶ人へ

単独(たんどく)の良(よ)さをいかし、自由に自分のペースでStep 1〜5を進んでください。自分で自分の進歩を見届(みとど)け、それぞれの目的(もくてき)や目標(もくひょう)、例(たと)えば入試(にゅうし)や検定(けんてい)試験(しけん)、会議(かいぎ)やプレゼンなどのために書く力を付(つ)けてください。

TAGAKI 20目標

メンタル	1か2か、肯定か否定か、はっきり決める

身近な話題について、1か2か、肯定か否定か、自分の考えをはっきり述べていくことを練習します。

英語	英語1文ではなく、3文で書く

英語1文だけではなく、3文程度（20語前後）で自分の言いたいことをはっきり表現しましょう。

書く 3〜5分で書きましょう。

Writing Time

1 ① I like to ... と ② I don't like to ... 自分はどちらかな？ どちらか選んで ① と ② を入れて全文を書こう。

```
I like to be active. I often
go out and ride a bike.
I sometimes go shopping.
It makes me really happy!
```

Step 3 Writing

自分が決めた Sample Sentences に、Words and Phrases A B から自分で選んだものを当てはめて全文を書き写しましょう。

---

2 上で書いた文を見ないで書いて、見ないで言おう。

```
I like to be active. I often go
out and ride a bike.
I sometimes go shopping.
It makes me really happy!
```

Step 4 Writing

Writing Time 1 で書いた文を見ないで、もう一度書きましょう。

伝える

Step 5 Speaking

Writing Time 2 で書いた文を覚えて声に出して言いましょう。

ペアやグループでTAGAKIを学ぶ人へ	Step 1〜5を進めた後、友達や家族、先生に向けて発表したり、他の人の発表を聞いて、英語または日本語でディスカッションしたりして、4技能の学習へ発展してください。書いたものは見ないで発表しましょう。

1 Personality 〈パーソナリティー〉

Active
アクティブな人

音声がきけます♪

Sample Sentences

1 I like to ...

I like to be active. I often go out and [A] _____. I sometimes [B] _____. It makes me really happy!

2 I don't like to ...

I don't like to be active. I don't go out and [A] _____. I don't [B] _____. Keep still!

Words and Phrases

よくすること / しないこと

[A]

❶ kick a ball ❷ ride a bike ❸ run/jog ❹ hang out with my friends

時どきすること / しないこと

[B]

❶ dance in the park ❷ get up very early ❸ clean the house ❹ go shopping

Writing Time

1 ⌐1¬ I like to ... と ⌐2¬ I don't like to ... 自分はどちらかな？　どちらか選んで Ⓐ と Ⓑ を入れて全文を書こう。

2 上で書いた文を見ないで書いて、見ないで言おう。

2

Life 〈生活・人生〉

Adulthood
大人の時

音声がきけます♪

Sample Sentences

1 | I think ...

I think life is more fun when you're an adult. I think an adult chooses **A** and has more **B** . Let's all act like grown-ups!

2 | I don't think ...

I don't think life is more fun when you're an adult. I don't think an adult chooses **A** and has more **B** . I want to stay a child forever!

Words and Phrases

大人が決めること / 決めないこと

A

❶ what to buy   ❷ where to live   ❸ what to do   ❹ when to take holidays

大人が持っているもの / 持っていないもの

B

❶ money   ❷ freedom   ❸ experience   ❹ ideas

Writing Time

1 [1] I think ... と [2] I don't think ... 自分はどちらかな？ どちらか選んで A と B を入れて全文を書こう。

2 上で書いた文を見ないで書いて、見ないで言おう。

3 Ants
アリタイプの人

音声がきけます♪

Sample Sentences

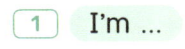 1 I'm ...

I'm an ant-type person. The ant says, "Work first and enjoy later." So I [A]   first and [B]   later. That's the way to go!

2 I'm not ...

I'm not an ant-type person. The ant says, "Work first and enjoy later." But I [A]   first and [B]   later. I'm easy going!

Words and Phrases

先にすること / 後ですること

A B

1 study　　2 do my homework　　3 prepare for tests　　4 clean my desk

5 play games　　6 read comic books　　7 check emails　　8 lie on the sofa

Writing Time

1 ① I'm ... と ② I'm not ... 自分はどちらかな？　どちらか選んで
Ⓐ 　　　　と Ⓑ 　　　　を入れて全文を書こう。

2 上で書いた文を見ないで書いて、見ないで言おう。

11

Personality 〈パーソナリティー〉

4 Airplanes
飛行機（ひこうき）

音声がきけます♪

Sample Sentences

1 When my family goes on a trip, **I want to ...**

When my family goes on a trip, I want to go by airplane. I think airplanes are [A] . I enjoy [B] . It's so great!

2 When my family goes on a trip, **I don't want to ...**

When my family goes on a trip, I don't want to go by airplane. I don't think airplanes are [A] . I don't enjoy [B] . I'm scared!

Words and Phrases

飛行機（ひこうき）について思うこと / 思わないこと

[A]
1. amazing
2. powerful
3. comfortable
4. safe

楽しめること / 楽しめないこと

[B]
1. eating and drinking
2. watching movies
3. watching the clouds down below
4. feeling like a big bird

Writing Time

1 When my family goes on a trip, [1] I want to ... と [2] I don't want to ... 自分はどちらかな？　どちらか選んで Ⓐ　　　と Ⓑ　　　を入れて全文を書こう。

2 上で書いた文を見ないで書いて、見ないで言おう。

5 Baking
おかし作り

Sample Sentences

1 I'm good at ...

I'm good at baking. I bake ⒶＡ．
So, I can make ⒷＢ happy. It's good, isn't it?

2 I'm not good at ...

I'm not good at baking. I don't bake ⒶＡ. So, I can't make ⒷＢ happy. I'm so sorry!

Words and Phrases

焼くもの / 焼かないもの

Ⓐ

① birthday cake

② apple pie

③ Christmas cake

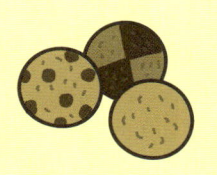
④ cookies

喜ぶ人 / 喜ばない人

Ⓑ

① my friends

② my family

③ my boyfriend /girlfriend

④ my grandpa /grandma

Writing Time

1 [1] I'm good at ... と [2] I'm not good at ... 自分はどちらかな？　どちらか選んで A と B を入れて全文を書こう。

....

....

....

....

2 上で書いた文を見ないで書いて、見ないで言おう。

....

....

....

....

6 Band
バンド

音声がきけます♪

Sample Sentences

1 I think ...

I think playing music together is a lot of fun. In the future, I'll play A _____. I'll join B _____. How cool!

2 I don't think ...

I don't think playing music together is a lot of fun. In the future, I won't play A _____. I won't join B _____. What a horrible noise!

Words and Phrases

将来、演奏したい楽器 / 演奏したくない楽器

A
❶ the guitar　❷ the trumpet　❸ the keyboard　❹ the saxophone

参加したいグループ / 参加したくないグループ

B
❶ a rock band　❷ a jazz band　❸ an ensemble　❹ a marching band

16

Writing Time

1 　①　 I think ...　と　②　 I don't think ...　自分はどちらかな？　どちらか選ん
で　Ⓐ　と　Ⓑ　を入れて全文を書こう。

2 　上で書いた文を見ないで書いて、見ないで言おう。

Life 〈生活・人生〉

Beautiful Morning

気持ちの良い朝

音声がきけます♪

Sample Sentences

1 In the morning, I wake up ...

In the morning, I wake up because of [A]＿＿＿. I open the windows [B]＿＿＿ I feel great!

2 In the morning, I don't wake up ...

In the morning, I don't wake up because of [A]＿＿＿. I don't open the windows [B]＿＿＿ I'm not a morning person.

Words and Phrases

目が覚める理由 / 覚めない理由

[A]

❶ the alarm clock　❷ the bright sun　❸ the birds outside　❹ feeling tired

窓を開けてすること / しないこと

[B]

❶ to say "Good morning!"　❷ to check the weather.　❸ to breathe the fresh air.　❹ to say "Hello, birds!"

Writing Time

1 In the morning, [1] I wake up ...  と [2] I don't wake up ...  自分はどちらかな？　どちらか選んで A　　　 と B　　 を入れて全文を書こう。

---

2 上で書いた文を見ないで書いて、見ないで言おう。

8 Bicycle Racing
自転車レース

音声がきけます♪

Sample Sentences

1 I'll go to ...

I'll go to [A]_____ to see the famous bicycle road race. It'll be [B]_____ to see the bicycle race. It's so cool!

2 I won't go to ...

I won't go to [A]_____ to see the famous bicycle road race. It won't be [B]_____ to see the bicycle race. I'll go eat ice cream instead.

Words and Phrases

行きたい国 / 行きたくない国

[A]

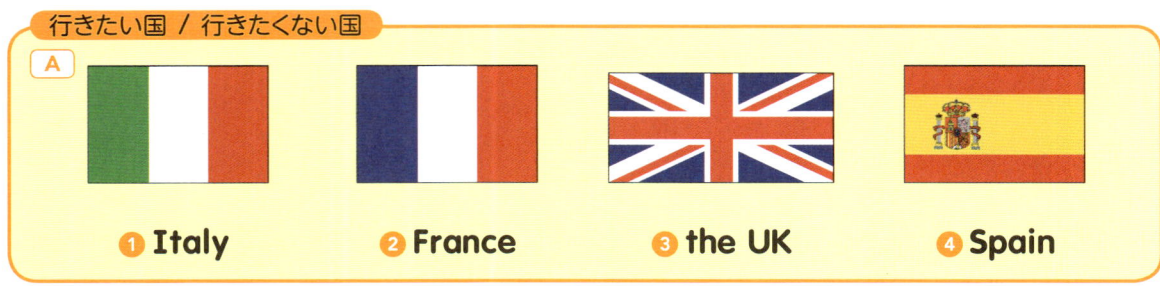

❶ Italy　　❷ France　　❸ the UK　　❹ Spain

どういうレースになるか / ならないか

[B]

❶ exciting　　❷ thrilling　　❸ surprising　　❹ amazing

Writing Time

1 ⬜1 I'll go to ... と ⬜2 I won't go to ... 自分はどちらかな？　どちらか選んで Ⓐ と Ⓑ を入れて全文を書こう。

2 上で書いた文を見ないで書いて、見ないで言おう。

9 Big Breakfast
たっぷりの朝ごはん

音声がきけます♪

Sample Sentences

1 I have ...

I have a big breakfast. It keeps me [A]_____. It wakes up [B]_____. A big breakfast makes a healthy body!

2 I don't have ...

I don't have a big breakfast. It doesn't keep me [A]_____. It doesn't wake up [B]_____. A light breakfast makes a light body!

Words and Phrases

たっぷり食べた時の状態 / 食べない時の状態

[A]
❶ healthy   ❷ smart   ❸ strong   ❹ awake

目覚める部分 / 目覚めない部分

[B]
❶ my brain   ❷ my whole body   ❸ my stomach   ❹ my muscles

Writing Time

1 ① I have ... と ② I don't have ... 自分はどちらかな？ どちらか選んで A と B を入れて全文を書こう。

2 上で書いた文を見ないで書いて、見ないで言おう。

10

Christmas
クリスマス

音声がきけます♪

Sample Sentences

1 I like ...

I like Christmas. Our town has
A _____. I like to B _____.
Merry Christmas!

2 I don't like ...

I don't like Christmas. Our town
doesn't have A _____. I don't like
to B _____. It's just another day!

Words and Phrases

街にあるもの / ないもの

A

❶ Christmas illuminations ❷ Christmas trees ❸ Christmas markets ❹ Christmas concerts

するのが好きなこと / 好きではないこと

B

❶ eat Christmas cake ❷ write Christmas cards ❸ choose Christmas presents ❹ have a Christmas party

Writing Time

1 [1] I like ... と [2] I don't like ... 自分はどちらかな?　どちらか選んで
Ⓐ　　と Ⓑ　　を入れて全文を書こう。

2 上で書いた文を見ないで書いて、見ないで言おう。

Places 〈場所〉

City
都会

音声がきけます♪

Sample Sentences

1 In the future, I'll live in ...

In the future, I'll live in a city. I'll enjoy [A]_____. I think cities have [B]_____. Cities are so exciting!

2 In the future, I won't live in ...

In the future, I won't live in a city. I won't enjoy [A]_____. I don't think cities have [B]_____. Cities are so noisy!

Words and Phrases

楽しむこと / 楽しまないこと

[A]
① a lot of events ② the freedom ③ my own lifestyle ④ all the different people

都会にあるもの / ないもの

[B]
① nice parks ② big movie theaters ③ lots of places to go ④ friendly shops

Writing Time

1 In the future, 1 I'll live in ... と 2 I won't live in ... 自分はどちらかな？　どちらか選んで Ⓐ と Ⓑ を入れて全文を書こう。

2 上で書いた文を見ないで書いて、見ないで言おう。

Cold Food
冷たい食べもの

音声がきけます♪

Sample Sentences

1   I like to ...

I like to eat something cold. ⒶＡ is my favorite food. Eating something cold makes me ⒷＢ. Come on, let's eat!

2   I don't like to ...

I don't like to eat something cold. ⒶＡ isn't my favorite food. On the other hand, eating something hot makes me ⒷＢ. Umm ... yum!

Words and Phrases

好きな冷たい食べもの / 好きではない冷たい食べもの

Ⓐ
❶ ice cream   ❷ cold pasta   ❸ cold soup   ❹ watermelon

食べると感じること

Ⓑ
❶ sleepy   ❷ feel heavy   ❸ feel great   ❹ happy

Writing Time

1 1 I like to ... と 2 I don't like to ... 自分はどちらかな？　どちらか選んで A ＿＿＿ と B ＿＿＿ を入れて全文を書こう。

＿＿＿＿＿＿＿＿＿＿＿＿＿＿＿＿＿＿＿＿＿＿＿＿＿＿

＿＿＿＿＿＿＿＿＿＿＿＿＿＿＿＿＿＿＿＿＿＿＿＿＿＿

＿＿＿＿＿＿＿＿＿＿＿＿＿＿＿＿＿＿＿＿＿＿＿＿＿＿

＿＿＿＿＿＿＿＿＿＿＿＿＿＿＿＿＿＿＿＿＿＿＿＿＿＿

2 上で書いた文を見ないで書いて、見ないで言おう。

＿＿＿＿＿＿＿＿＿＿＿＿＿＿＿＿＿＿＿＿＿＿＿＿＿＿

＿＿＿＿＿＿＿＿＿＿＿＿＿＿＿＿＿＿＿＿＿＿＿＿＿＿

＿＿＿＿＿＿＿＿＿＿＿＿＿＿＿＿＿＿＿＿＿＿＿＿＿＿

＿＿＿＿＿＿＿＿＿＿＿＿＿＿＿＿＿＿＿＿＿＿＿＿＿＿

Personality 〈パーソナリティー〉

Eating Things First

音声がきけます♪

先に食べる

Sample Sentences

1 I eat ...

I eat my favorite food first, because [A] . This way, my favorite food tastes [B] ! I want to eat it again!

2 I don't eat ...

I don't eat my favorite food first, even though [A] . Still, my favorite food tastes [B] ! I save the best for last.

Words and Phrases

好きなものから先に食べる理由 / 食べない理由

[A]

1 someone else might take it
2 the food will get cold
3 I like it
4 I want to enjoy my meal

先に食べるとどうか / 食べないとどうか

[B]

1 wonderful
2 delicious
3 better
4 special

Writing Time

1 1 I eat ... と 2 I don't eat ... 自分はどちらかな? どちらか選んで A と B を入れて全文を書こう。

....

....

....

....

2 上で書いた文を見ないで書いて、見ないで言おう。

....

....

....

....

Eco Style
エコスタイル

音声がきけます♪

Sample Sentences

1 I'm interested in ...

I'm interested in eco style. I try to [A] _____ things, because I'm very worried about [B] _____ . What a good global citizen!

2 I'm not interested in ...

I'm not interested in eco style. I don't try to [A] _____ things, because I'm not too worried about [B] _____ . Should I think about it more?

Words and Phrases

努力していること / していないこと

[A]
❶ recycle　❷ reduce　❸ reuse　❹ refuse

心配していること / していないこと

[B]
❶ global warming　❷ climate change　❸ water pollution　❹ air pollution

Writing Time

1 ① I'm interested in ... と ② I'm not interested in ... 自分はどちらかな?
どちらか選んで Ⓐ と Ⓑ を入れて全文を書こう。

2 上で書いた文を見ないで書いて、見ないで言おう。

15 First Day of School

学校の初めての日

音声がきけます♪

Sample Sentences

1 I remember ...

I remember my first day of elementary school. I remember A＿＿＿. I was very B＿＿＿. Time flies!

2 I don't remember ...

I don't remember my first day of elementary school. I don't remember A＿＿＿. I wasn't very B＿＿＿. It was a long time ago!

Words and Phrases

覚えていること / 覚えていないこと

A
① meeting my new teachers
② carrying my new school bag
③ wearing my new shoes
④ meeting my new friends

その時の気持ち

B
① excited
② happy
③ nervous
④ shy

Writing Time

1 〔1〕 I remember ... と 〔2〕 I don't remember ... 自分はどちらかな？　どちらか選^{えら}んで Ⓐ と Ⓑ を入れて全文を書こう。

（解答欄）

2 上で書いた文を見ないで書いて、見ないで言おう。

（解答欄）

16

Highest Places

高いところ

Sample Sentences

[1] Someday, I want to ...

Someday, I want to go to one of the highest places on the earth. I'll go to [A]⬚. It's over 8,000 meters high. I'll see [B]⬚. How thrilling!

[2] I don't want to ...

I don't want to go to any of the highest places on the earth. I won't go to [A]⬚. It's over 8,000 meters high. I don't want to see [B]⬚ there. How scary!

Words and Phrases

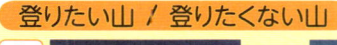
登りたい山 / 登りたくない山

[A]

❶ Mount Everest ❷ Mount Lhotse ❸ Mount Manaslu ❹ Mount Godwin-Austen (K2)

見えるもの / 見たくないもの

[B]

❶ everything below ❷ a beautiful landscape ❸ a sky full of stars ❹ shining snow and ice

Writing Time

1 ① Someday, I want to ... と ② I don't want to ... 自分はどちらかな?
どちらか選<ruby>選<rt>えら</rt></ruby>んで Ⓐ と Ⓑ を入れて全文を書こう。

2 上で書いた文を見ないで書いて、見ないで言おう。

17

Hotel Reception Robots

ホテルの受付ロボット

音声がきけます♪

Sample Sentences

1 Hotel reception robots are ...

Hotel reception robots are wonderful. I think they can [A]_____. I want them to [B]_____. Welcome!

2 Hotel reception robots aren't ...

Hotel reception robots aren't wonderful. I don't think they can [A]_____. I don't want them to [B]_____. "O-Mo-Te-Na-Shi", please!

Words and Phrases

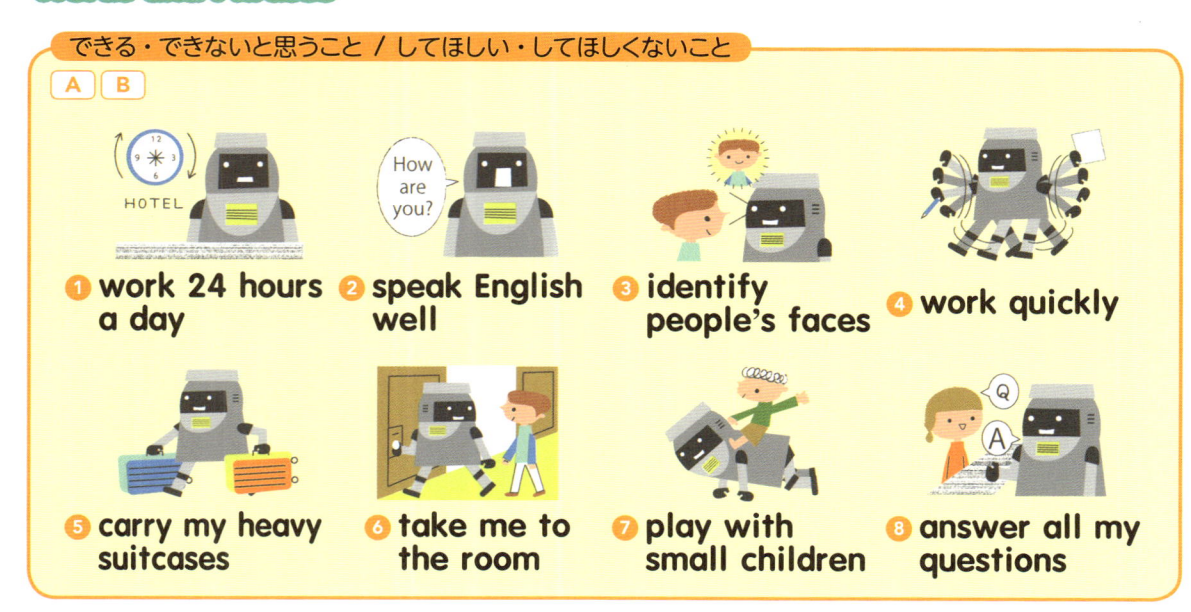

できる・できないと思うこと / してほしい・してほしくないこと

A B

1 work 24 hours a day
2 speak English well
3 identify people's faces
4 work quickly
5 carry my heavy suitcases
6 take me to the room
7 play with small children
8 answer all my questions

Writing Time

1 ① Hotel reception robots are … と ② Hotel reception robots aren't …

自分はどちらかな？　どちらか選んで A　　　 と B　　　 を入れて全文を書こう。

---

2 上で書いた文を見ないで書いて、見ないで言おう。

18

Indoors
インドア派

音声がきけます♪

Sample Sentences

1 I'm happy ...

I'm happy when [A] at home. I choose to be indoors a lot. I like to stay [B] . Let's relax!

2 I'm not happy ...

I'm not happy when [A] at home. I don't choose to be indoors a lot. I don't like to stay [B] . Let's go outside!

Words and Phrases

家で楽しいと感じること / 楽しいと感じないこと

[A]

❶ I'm on the sofa ❷ I'm in my room ❸ I'm on the bed ❹ I play games

いるのが好きな場所 / 好きではない場所

[B]

❶ in a quiet place ❷ in the library ❸ in the bathtub ❹ on the porch

Writing Time

1 ① I'm happy ... と ② I'm not happy ... 自分はどちらかな？　どちらか
選んで Ⓐ　　　と Ⓑ　　　を入れて全文を書こう。

2 上で書いた文を見ないで書いて、見ないで言おう。

Personality 〈パーソナリティー〉

Kings and Queens

王様と女王様

音声がきけます♪

Sample Sentences

1 I want to ...

I want to be a king/queen. I want to ⒶＡ ＿＿＿ and I want to have ⒷＢ ＿＿＿. The world is all mine!

2 I don't want to ...

I don't want to be a king/queen. I don't want to ⒶＡ ＿＿＿ and I don't want to have ⒷＢ ＿＿＿. It's my life!

Words and Phrases

したいこと / したくないこと

Ａ
① be at the top ② decide everything ③ give orders ④ meet famous people

持ちたいもの / 持ちたくないもの

Ｂ
① many servants ② a lot of money ③ a huge castle ④ my own jet

Writing Time

1 1 I want to ... と 2 I don't want to ... 自分はどちらかな？　どちら
か選んで A　　 と B　　 を入れて全文を書こう。（king か queen も選ぼう。）

2 上で書いた文を見ないで書いて、見ないで言おう。

20 Listeners

聞き上手な人

音声がきけます♪

Sample Sentences

1 I'm ...

I'm a good listener. I don't ⒜ [   ].
And I listen ⒝ [   ]. I'm glad I'm a
good listener. I'll keep listening!

2 I'm not ...

I'm not a good listener. I ⒜ [   ].
And I don't listen ⒝ [   ]. I want
to be a good listener. I should
listen more.

Words and Phrases

しないこと / すること

Ⓐ
❶ talk a lot　❷ speak loudly　❸ make people laugh　❹ speak fast

話を聞く相手 / 聞かない相手

Ⓑ 6-2

❶ to my classmates　❷ to everybody　❸ to my parents　❹ to my brother/sister

Writing Time

1 [1] I'm ... と [2] I'm not ... 自分はどちらかな? どちらか選んで [A] と [B] を入れて全文を書こう。

2 上で書いた文を見ないで書いて、見ないで言おう。

21 Sport 〈スポーツ〉

Marathon

マラソン大会

音声がきけます♪

Sample Sentences

1 I think ...

I think the marathon is [A] sport. In the future, I want to [E] . Go! Go! Go!

2 I don't think ...

I don't think the marathon is [A] sport. In the future, I don't want to [B] . The marathon takes too long!

Words and Phrases

マラソンについて思うこと / 思わないこと

[A]

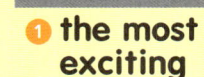

❶ the most exciting   ❷ the most enjoyable   ❸ the most popular   ❹ the best

将来したいこと / したくないこと

[B]

❶ work as a volunteer   ❷ watch the race on TV   ❸ cheer the runners on the street   ❹ enter the race as a runner

Writing Time

1 ① I think ... と ② I don't think ... 自分はどちらかな？ どちらか選んで A と B を入れて全文を書こう。

2 上で書いた文を見ないで書いて、見ないで言おう。

22 Mars
火星

音声がきけます♪

Sample Sentences

1 If I go to Mars, I want to ...

If I go to Mars, I want to [A]_____.
And I want to bring back [B]_____.
I want to go right now!

2 Even if I go to Mars, I don't want to ...

Even if I go to Mars, I don't want to [A]_____. And I don't want to bring back [B]_____. There's no place like Earth!

Words and Phrases

火星に行ったらしたいこと / したくないこと

[A]
1 meet the Martians 2 put a flag up 3 make a movie 4 drive around

持って帰りたいもの / 帰りたくないもの

[B]
1 some photos 2 a Martian 3 some sounds 4 some rocks

Writing Time

1 If/Even if I go to Mars, 1 I want to ... と 2 I don't want to ... 自分はどちらかな？　どちらか選んで A と B を入れて全文を書こう。

2 上で書いた文を見ないで書いて、見ないで言おう。

23

Meat
肉

音声がきけます♪

Sample Sentences

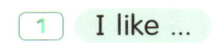

1 I like ...

I like my steak ⒜⬛⬛⬛. I love eating steak. Eating meat will ⒝⬛⬛⬛. Bravo, meat!

2 I don't like ...

I don't like my steak ⒜⬛⬛⬛. I don't like eating steak. Eating meat won't ⒝⬛⬛⬛. I'm a vegetarian!

Words and Phrases

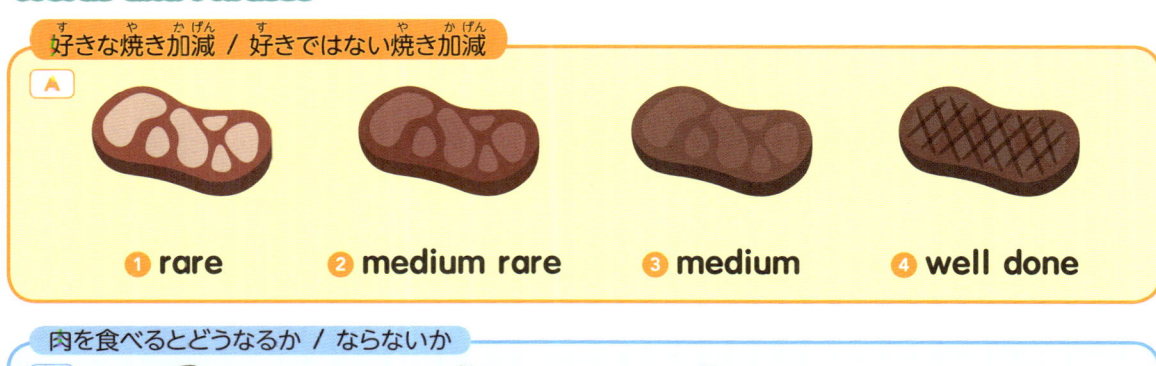

好きな焼き加減 / 好きではない焼き加減

⒜

❶ rare ❷ medium rare ❸ medium ❹ well done

肉を食べるとどうなるか / ならないか

⒝

❶ make me healthy ❷ make my muscles strong ❸ make me feel good ❹ increase the iron in my blood

Writing Time

1 ⃞1 I like ... と ⃞2 I don't like ... 自分はどちらかな？ どちらか選んで

Ⓐ と Ⓑ を入れて全文を書こう。

---

2 上で書いた文を見ないで書いて、見ないで言おう。

24

Personality 〈パーソナリティー〉

Nightmares

こわい夢

音声がきけます♪

Sample Sentences

1　I was so scared that ...

A chased me. I was so scared that I tried to B . But I couldn't. Sooo scary!

2　But I wasn't scared, ...

A chased me. But I wasn't scared, so I didn't try to B . You can't scare me!

Words and Phrases

追いかけてきたこわいもの / こわくないもの

A

❶ a ghost　❷ a zombie　❸ a black shadow　❹ a huge lion

やろうとしたこと / しなかったこと

B

❶ scream　❷ wake up　❸ jump out of my bed　❹ call someone

Writing Time

1 ① I was so scared that ... と ② But I wasn't scared, ... 自分はどちら
かな？　どちらか選んで Ⓐ　　　と Ⓑ　　　を入れて全文を書こう。

2 上で書いた文を見ないで書いて、見ないで言おう。

Personality 〈パーソナリティー〉

Pets
ペット

音声がきけます♪

Sample Sentences

1 I have ...

I have my own pet, because I like to 〔A〕_____. Having a pet is 〔B〕_____. Stay with me forever!

2 I don't have ...

I don't have my own pet, because I don't like to 〔A〕_____. Having a pet isn't 〔B〕_____. That's the way I like it!

Words and Phrases

するのが好きなこと / 好きではないこと

〔A〕
❶ take care of it ❷ sleep with it ❸ play with it ❹ feed it

ペットを飼う理由 / 飼わない理由

〔B〕
❶ interesting ❷ exciting ❸ fun ❹ cool

Writing Time

1 ⬛ ① I have ... と ② I don't have ... 自分はどちらかな？　どちらか選ん
で Ⓐ と Ⓑ を入れて全文を書こう。

2 上で書いた文を見ないで書いて、見ないで言おう。

Music 〈音楽〉

26 Rhythm
リズム

音声がきけます♪

Sample Sentences

1 I love ...

I love playing Ⓐ   . I want to make a lot of noise. It's really Ⓑ   ! Whooooo! Bang! Bang! Bang!

2 I don't like ...

I don't like playing Ⓐ   . I don't want to make a lot of noise. It's not really Ⓑ   ! Shh! How annoying!

Words and Phrases

Ⓐ 演奏するのが大好きな楽器 / 好きではない楽器

❶ the drums   ❷ the bongo drums   ❸ the cymbals   ❹ the Japanese drums

Ⓑ 音を出すとどうなるか / ならないか

❶ fun   ❷ exciting   ❸ cool   ❹ interesting

Writing Time

1 ① I love ... と ② I don't like ... 自分はどちらかな？　どちらか選んで Ⓐ　　　と Ⓑ　　　を入れて全文を書こう。

2 上で書いた文を見ないで書いて、見ないで言おう。

27 Salty

しょっぱいもの

音声がきけます♪

Sample Sentences

1 My favorite snacks are ...

My favorite snacks are salty things like [A] _____ . I need salty food, whenever I feel [B] _____ . Crunch, crunch!

2 My favorite snacks aren't ...

My favorite snacks aren't salty things like [A] _____ . I don't need salty food, even if I feel [B] _____ . Give me sweets!

Words and Phrases

好きなしょっぱいスナック / 好きではないしょっぱいスナック

[A]

❶ chips   ❷ popcorn   ❸ rice crackers   ❹ salted nuts

いつもこんな時にほしい / こんな時でさえほしくない

[B]

❶ stressed   ❷ tired   ❸ sick   ❹ lonely

Writing Time

1 ① My favorite snacks are ... と ② My favorite snacks aren't ... 自分は どちらかな？　どちらか選んで A　　　と B　　　を入れて全文を書こう。

....

....

....

....

2 上で書いた文を見ないで書いて、見ないで言おう。

....

....

....

....

28 Sky

空

音声がきけます♪

Sample Sentences

1 I enjoy ...

I enjoy looking at the sky. I think the sky is the most beautiful ⒶＡ . The sky is also very beautiful ⒷＢ . What a wonderful world!

2 I don't enjoy ...

I don't enjoy looking at the sky. I don't think the sky is beautiful ⒶＡ . The sky isn't beautiful ⒷＢ . The sky is boring.

Words and Phrases

一番きれいだと思う時間帯・季節 / きれいだと思わない時間帯・季節

Ⓐ **❶** in the morning **❷** in the afternoon **❸** in spring/autumn (fall) **❹** in summer/winter

空にあるときれいなもの / きれいでないもの

Ⓑ **❶** with clouds **❷** with a rainbow **❸** with sunlight **❹** with snow

Writing Time

1 [1] I enjoy ... と [2] I don't enjoy ... 自分はどちらかな？　どちらか選んで A と B を入れて全文を書こう。

---

2 上で書いた文を見ないで書いて、見ないで言おう。

School Life 〈学校生活〉

29 Winning and Losing

勝ちと負け

音声がきけます♪

Sample Sentences

1 Last year, | our class won ...

Last year, our class won [A]

because we practiced so hard. So

we feel [B] about it. We're the

best!

2 Last year, | our class lost ...

Last year, our class lost [A]

although we practiced so hard. Even

today, we feel [B] about it. We

should practice harder next time!

Words and Phrases

勝った試合 / 負けた試合

[A]

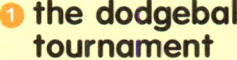

❶ the dodgeball tournament   ❷ the volleyball tournament   ❸ the soccer tournament   ❹ the long jump rope tournament

思い出す感情

[B]

❶ happy   ❷ excited   ❸ sorry   ❹ sad

Writing Time

1 Last year, [1] our class won ... と [2] our class lost ... 自分はどちらかな？　どちらか選んで [A] と [B] を入れて全文を書こう。

----

2 上で書いた文を見ないで書いて、見ないで言おう。

30 Life 〈生活・人生〉

Winter Vacation
冬休み

音声がきけます♪

Sample Sentences

1 At the beginning of winter vacation, I always make up my mind to ...

At the beginning of winter vacation, I always make up my mind to [A]____. I make [B]____ happy. I'm almost perfect!

2 At the beginning of winter vacation, I don't make up my mind to ...

At the beginning of winter vacation, I don't make up my mind to [A]____. I don't make [B]____ happy. Nobody is perfect.

Words and Phrases

いつも決心すること / 決心しないこと

[A]
❶ clean up my room
❷ finish my homework
❸ go to bed early
❹ do the chores

幸せにする人 / しない人

[B]
❶ my mom
❷ my dad
❸ my grandma/ grandpa
❹ myself

Writing Time

1 At the beginning of winter vacation, 1 **I always make up my mind to ...** と 2

I don't make up my mind to ... 自分はどちらかな？　どちらか選んで A

と B 　を入れて全文を書こう。

---

2 上で書いた文を見ないで書いて、見ないで言おう。

コードを読み取れない方や音声をダウンロードしたい方は、右のQRコードまたは
以下のURLより、アクセスしてください。
https://www.mpi-j.co.jp/contents/shop/mpi/contents/digital/tagaki20.html

TAGAKI® 20

発 行 日 ●	2018年10月11日　初版第 1 刷　　2023年 1 月20日　第16刷
	2024年 3 月 1 日　 2 版第 2 刷
執　　　　筆 ●	松香洋子
執 筆 協 力 ●	近藤理恵子
英 文 校 正 ●	Glenn McDougall
編　　　　集 ●	株式会社カルチャー・プロ
イ ラ ス ト ●	池田蔵人　石井里果　小林昌子　サノエミコ　仲西太　武曽宏幸
本文デザイン ●	DB Works
本 文 組 版 ●	株式会社内外プロセス
録 音・ 編 集 ●	一般財団法人英語教育協議会（ELEC）
ナレーション ●	Howard Colefield　Julia Yermakov
写 真 提 供 ●	アフロ
協　　　　力 ●	赤松由梨　粕谷みゆき　貞野浩子　野中美恵　宮下いづみ　山内由紀子
印　　　　刷 ●	シナノ印刷株式会社
発　　　　行 ●	株式会社mpi松香フォニックス
	〒151-0053
	東京都渋谷区代々木2-16-2 第二甲田ビル 2F
	fax:03-5302-1652
	URL:https://www.mpi-j.co.jp

＊本書で取り扱っている内容は、2017年までの情報をもとに作成しています。
＊QRコードは（株）デンソーウェーブの登録商標です。